Room by Room Storage Solutions

Monte Burch

BETTERWAY HOME
CINCINNATI, OHIO
www.fwmedia.com

Distributed in Canada by Fraser Direct
100 Armstrong Avenue
Georgetown, Ontario L7G 5S4
Canada

Distributed in the U.K. and Europe by David & Charles
Brunel House
Newton Abbot
Devon TQ12 4PU
England
Tel: (+44) 1626 323200
Fax: (+44) 1626 323319
E-mail: postmaster@davidandcharles.co.uk

Distributed in Australia by Capricorn Link
P.O. Box 704
Windsor, NSW 2756
Australia

Visit our Web site at www.popularwoodworking.com.

13   12   11   10   09   5   4   3   2   1

Library of Congress Cataloging-in-Publication Data

Burch, Monte.
  Room by room / by Monte Burch. -- 1st ed.
      p. cm.
  Includes index.
  ISBN 978-1-55870-870-9 (pbk. : alk. paper)
  1. Storage in the home. I. Title.
  TX309.B87 2009
  643'.5--dc22
                        2008049227

METRIC CONVERSION CHART

To Convert	To	Multiply By
Inches	Centimeters	2.54
Centimeters	Inches	0.4
Feet	Centimeters	30.5
Centimeters	Feet	0.03
Yards	Meters	0.9
Meters	Yards	1.1

ACQUISITIONS EDITOR: David Thiel
SENIOR EDITOR: Jim Stack
DESIGNER: Brian Roeth
PRODUCTION COORDINATOR: Mark Griffin
ILLUSTRATOR: Jim Stack

ABOUT THE AUTHOR

Monte Burch was an editor for *Workbench* magazine through the late 1960s and early 1970s. He has been a freelance how-to and woodworking writer/photographer/ illustrator and is the author of thousands of magazine articles and over 70 how-to, outdoor and other non-fiction books, including a number that were *Popular Science* monthly main selections, such as the *Home Cabinetmaker* and *Complete Guide to Building Log Homes*. Over a million copies of his books have been sold. His latest book is *Tool School, The missing manual for your tools* by *Betterway* books. Monte is a founding member of the National Association of Home and Workshop Writers, and lives on a 350-acre farm where he has a full woodworking shop and studio.

Contents

Organize Your Stuff

Even if we don't like to admit it, most of us have too much stuff. Your cabinets, closets, garage, attic or basement areas are probably disorganized, with items not stored properly, which can damage them, create stress in locating what you need and even cause an unsafe situation. The first step in storing your stuff is to cut the clutter and organize it. This usually means getting rid of some stuff. It's important to have a plan.

STEPS TO ORGANIZING

Step one is listing your items. Two is determining what you want to keep or get rid of and disposing of all unwanted items. Three is organizing the items you wish to keep and finding space/products to hold the items. Do this one room at a time and don't rush. In many instances you will be adding or installing organization products.

Make a list of what you have or need in a room or area. Make piles of like items, i.e., shoes. Then go through each pile and separate into three piles — definite keep, maybe keep and discard. The first pile you can usually set aside for organization and storage. Leave the second pile until last. The third, get-rid-of pile requires organization.

DONATE, SELL, DUMP OR RECYCLE

Depending on the items in the discard pile, you may wish to dump, donate or sell them. Some items can be recycled into more useful items and donating to a charity, local churches or community groups is an excellent choice. The Salvation Army (www.salvationarmyusa.org) and Goodwill (www.goodwill.org) organizations will take a wide range of items. They will give you a receipt for the value of your donation to be used for a tax deduction. On-line sources include www.freecycle.org and www.craigslist.org.

ABOVE **Clear plastic storage containers are great for storing things because you can see what you have in them.**

RIGHT **Wire shelves hang on standards that can be attached to any wall as needed.**

Scrap metal, old appliances and electronics are harder to dispose. Check local yellow pages for junk or scrap-metal dealers. You will be paid by the pound, depending on the metal involved. Larger retailers such as Office Depot, Staples or Best Buy may offer recycling of old computers, TVs and cell phones. Check out the Electronics Industries Alliance website, www.eiae.org.

The traditional yard or garage sale is a good way to sell your "stuff". Local newspapers often include a free yard-sale kit with signs when you advertise with them. Many newspapers offer free on-line classified ads for personal sales. On-line auctions such as E-Bay are good choices for unusual and/or collector items.

Some less-used or less-worn clothing and accessories can be taken to consignment shops. These shops specialize in specifics, such as kids, baby items, clothing, sporting goods and equipment. Clothing should be seasonal, clean and usually no more than one year old. You'll usually receive 40 to 50 percent of the selling price. If they don't sell within 60 days, you get them back. Flea-markets offer booths (for a price) where you can display just about anything and everything for sale.

Consider recycling. Old furniture pieces can be painted, antiqued and given a new life. Some can be changed into other types of storage.

FINAL ORGANIZATION AND STORAGE

Back to the second pile of "maybes". Separate clothing that is more than three years old. If you didn't wear it this past season, don't store it for next season. The same thing is true for shoes, except for sporting shoes still in good shape. Take a serious look at other items. If you didn't use them last season, they need to be discarded.

After getting rid of the unwanted, go back to the "keep" pile and organize it into separate piles, i.e., winter clothing, summer clothing and summer or winter sports equipment. Organize by the seasons. Now you can determine your organized storage needs. Items can be stored in tubs, hung on racks, stored on shelves and maybe pest-proof bags. With a storage plan in mind, you can shop for organizing products.

If you're having trouble deciding how to get rid of and organize your stuff, professionals are available for fees ranging from $50 to $150 an hour. They can help you decide whether to donate, sell or discard. For more information: National Association of Professional Organizers, www.napo.net.

Kitchen

One room in the home that benefits the most from organization is the kitchen. The kitchen is usually where the most work is done in the house, and it's important to have an easy-working kitchen with efficient storage space. In the past, experienced cabinetmakers custom-designed kitchen cabinets to suit the owner's needs as well as their cooking style. Now individually manufactured units are combined to create a full set of cabinets. In either instance, it's important to design the kitchen to suit your family, and create a well-organized storage system. If you're building or remodeling, you have the perfect opportunity to create an efficient kitchen. Your old kitchen can also be made more efficient with a creative use of the space available. One of the more important factors in kitchen design is the efficient location of the cabinets to prevent unnecessary steps and overreaching.

Kitchen Storage Solutions

A kitchen consists of three basic work areas: The *food storage* area includes not only the refrigerator, but a pantry cabinet or storage area for groceries coming into the kitchen. A corner cabinet with rotating shelves is an excellent choice for storage of canned goods. Or you may prefer a walk-in or customized storage pantry in another room. Make sure you observe which way your refrigerator door swings and allow clearance for the door to swing when designing the cabinets. The second is the *cooking* area. A wide choice of stove/oven ranges is available, as well as countertop cooking units and separate cabinet-held ovens. A microwave/convection oven or dual-oven unit are important cooking appliances. The third area is the *clean-up section*. The sink cabinet provides storage for supplies, tools used for preparing foods and for clean-up. The area can have a garbage disposal and dishwasher. The dishwasher should be located next to the sink with utensil and dish storage close to the dishwasher and table.

1 One of the more unusual kitchen storage products is the Rev-A-Shelf Chrome Blind Corner Optimizer. These replace the lazy Susan style organizers and take corner organization to a whole new level.

2 Easily installed, the Optimizer features four baskets on sliding racks. The first two racks are pulled straight out into the kitchen.

3 The first two racks are then slid to the side.

4 And the rear two racks are pulled out giving you easy access to all items stored in a usually hard-to-get-to corner of the kitchen.

OPPOSITE **Kitchens require organization and lots of storage. Efficient use of cabinets and proper design creates an easy working kitchen. Style and décor is also important in the kitchen where you spend a great deal of your time.**

ABOVE A kitchen consists of three basic work areas: food storage, cooking area and clean-up section.

RIGHT A pullout can be attached to a shelf for additional use of space below the shelf.

FAR RIGHT Pull-out racks are available to hold a wide variety of items.

ABOVE **The Rev-A-Shelf spice rack is easy to assemble and install with just a drill and screwdriver.**

ABOVE RIGHT **Specialized pull-outs are designed to hold specific items. A skillet rack holds skillets and lids.**

RIGHT **Drawer organizers are also important in kitchen efficiency.**

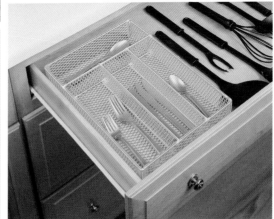

Kitchen Cabinets

Kitchen cabinets are individual units assembled to create a total kitchen. Many offer built-in storage solutions and a wide range of after-market kitchen organization products are available. They include the hardware to build in storage organization for those who have the skills and tools. Most are easily assembled and installed, usually with a screwdriver, a small electric drill, bits and a hammer.

One of the most common and useful items is lazy Susan rotating racks used to fill corner cabinets. The lazy Susan can be made with wood, polymer or stainless-steel shelves to suit a wide range of décor. They include a variety of shapes, including: full circle, kidney, D-shape, pie-cut and half-moon designs. The better products have independently operating shelves. The easiest ones to install feature a Twist-N-Lock support rod system. Full-circle units fill the entire cabinet and can be reached from the door on either side of the corner cabinet. D-shape units are made to fit corner cabinets with a single, center door. Pie-cuts are used on cabinet corners without upright stiles. The corner doors are fastened in place to the edges of the shelves with the doors rotating back into the cabinet as the shelf is turned. Even blind corner cabinets can utilize the half-moon style. These units fasten to one corner door and open out into the room as the door is opened. One of the more unusual units is the Rev-A-Shelf Chrome Blind Corner Optimizer. These take corner organization to a whole new level. The optimizer front baskets pull-out, then slide over to allow the rear baskets to be pulled out for total access to the stored items. Smaller units are available for upper cabinet corners.

TODAY, IN-CABINET STORAGE UNITS ARE NOT JUST THE OLD UTILITARIAN DESIGN. THEY ARE AVAILABLE IN WOOD, IN METAL OF WHITE, STAINLESS STEEL, CHROME AND BRUSHED-METAL FINISHES.

LEFT **Mesh storage bins are attractive and practical.**

Today in-cabinet storage units are not just the old utilitarian design. They are available in wood, in metal of white, stainless steel, chrome and brushed-metal finishes. The most popular organizers are pull-out trays, shelves and baskets. Cabinet accessories include: door-mounted cutting boards, bottom-mount waste containers, spice racks and stemware racks. Drawer organizers are important in cabinet organization and a wide range of products is available.

Cabinet pull-outs have become popular cabinet organizers. These slide into the cabinet for storage, pull out and provide organized storage. The Rev-A-Shelf base-cabinet pull-outs feature adjustable shelves with chrome rails to help keep everything in place. Made from birch or maple, with a UV clear-coat finish, they'll match any kitchen décor. The units glide on patented "tri-slides" minimizing any side-to-side motion — providing stability when pulled out. Door-mounted brackets provide up to five inches of flexibility and micro door adjustments and are designed for 9-, 12-, and 15-inch full-height face-frame base cabinets and 9-inch full-height frameless cabinets. The tall Rev-A-Shelf stainless-steel pull-out filler provides storage space behind decorative door panels. The filler comes in 39- and 45-inch heights and can be used with others to meet 84-, 90- or 96-inch height requirements. The units have magnetic, stainless-steel panels, chrome accents, accessory hooks or adjustable shelves with chrome rails, 150 pound-rated, full-extension ball bearing slides, mounting bracket and a three-slide design.

Kitchen Layout

These five, basic kitchen layouts are based on a triangular system of the three areas listed above. The total length of the triangle between the three areas should be no more than 22 feet for an efficiently designed kitchen.

One layout is the in-line, with all cabinets and appliances lined up against one wall. This is a common design in apartments where space is limited and is often used in conjunction with a dining area on the opposite wall. An in-line layout should only be used on short walls, as stretching the cabinets down a long wall means more steps and an inefficient kitchen.

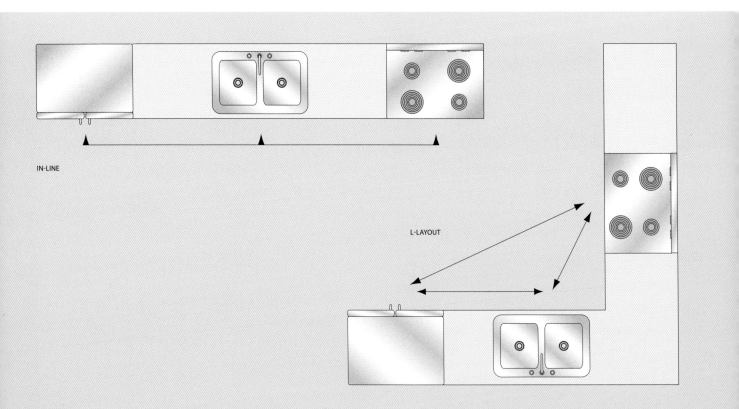

IN-LINE

L-LAYOUT

The L-layout (lower opposite page) is popular in larger kitchen areas. This design arranges the counters and appliances along two adjacent walls and is one of the most efficient designs because the work triangle is not crossed by other traffic. Space along the two other walls can be used for an eating area, laundry or family room arrangement.

The U-layout is an extension of the L-shape and is even more efficient as it provides more storage and work space in a smaller area. It is very useful in smaller kitchens. Placing one of the work areas on each wall with proper counter and storage space by each is convenient. Rotating shelves in the corner cabinets make good use of those areas. The peninsula kitchen is a variation of the U-shape and is often used to provide a room divider or bar between the kitchen and family or dining room.

The island design incorporates many styles. This is a cabinet placed in the center of the kitchen, with other appliances and cabinets arranged in a U or L shape around it. The island cabinet may feature a stove, sink or cutting surface for the gourmet cook.

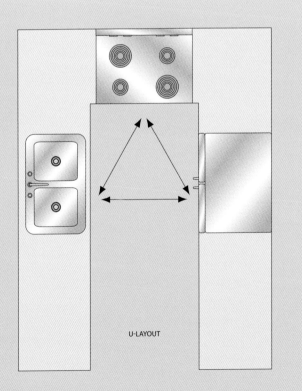

U-LAYOUT

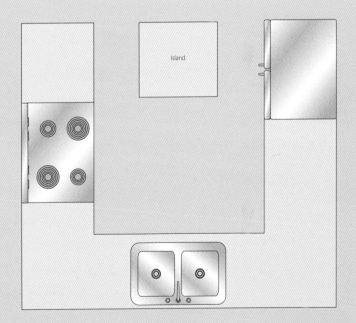

Island

ISLAND

The center cabinet may be entirely one height or may include a raised bar section for eating or as a room divider.

Another style is the "Pullman" or corridor layout. In this layout the cabinets, countertops and appliances are lined up on facing walls. This layout is primarily used in a long, narrow room and often has a dining area on one end of the kitchen. This layout must be at least eight-feet wide to allow sufficient floor space in the corridor.

Any of these layouts can include an infinite number of variations and combinations to suit your needs and to fit the available space.

In addition to the standardized layouts of kitchens, the cabinets are standardized. They consist of four types: wall, base, oven or tall units and specialty units such as desks. Cabinet sizes are standardized in height and depth and to suit standard appliance sizes. I have custom built cabinets to fit unusual wall heights, as well as for very tall or short people. Kitchens for handicapped persons are often individually designed,

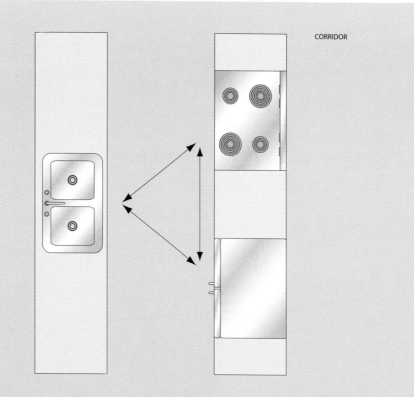

CORRIDOR

however, ready-made cabinets can be adapted. For instance, Rev-A-Shelf and Rubber-maid have wall-cabinet inserts that allow the upper cabinet items to be brought into reach of the wheel-chair bound.

NEW-KITCHEN LAYOUT

If you're starting with new cabinetry, use grid paper to create a sketch of the kitchen dimensions and sketch in the cabinetry you want. In many instances, builders or building supply stores can help you design the cabinets to suit your building, space and needs. But first, starting at one corner of the room, carefully measure the area with a metal, measuring tape and draw a rough, free-hand sketch. It's a good idea to measure everything in inches. Measure the countertop height from the floor, all appliances and around every door and window. Always measure the outside of window and door casings and make a note of these widths.

After measuring, make a second check of your measurements. Indicate all existing electrical outlets, plumbing pipes, radiators or other items that may effect the location of equipment or which you may wish to change. Transfer this sketch to paper with a grid. Each grid equals one foot. You should also measure the ceiling height and make up a scaled elevation drawing of the cabinets. This will help in determining exactly how they will look in accordance with room size. When making the drawing, allow one-half inch of additional space for dishwashers, ranges, trash compactors, washers and other appliances. You should also allow a minimum of three inches additional space around the refrigerator or freezer for air circulation. Kitchen cabinets not only provide storage space, but also some counter working space. Minimum counter spaces are considered to be 24 inches on either side of the sink and 15 inches by the door-opening side of a refrigerator or next to a built-in oven.

In addition to proper cabinet design, proper design of the storage space is important. Many of today's cabinets come with built-in and custom-storage areas such as spice racks, wine-glass holders and a variety of shelves. In addition, a wide range of easy-to-install storage systems are also available.

Pantry

Pantries provide additional storage space and working areas, if organized and arranged properly. Pantry storage can be part of a kitchen design, or a separate room next to the kitchen. A wide range of pantry-style cabinets are available, as a check with your local Lowe's or Home Depot stores will illustrate. Most are full height (from floor to ceiling) or with their tops level with standard wall-cabinet tops. Some units feature swing out or roll-out shelves, with several layers of narrow shelves for storing items such as canned goods. Others have pull-out shelves for deeper storage. Rev-A-Shelf has unique full-height pull-out pantry-style storage as well as a base-cabinet pantry unit. Kitchen pantry storage can be created in unusual places by inventive architects, cabinetmakers

MANY FAMILIES ARE DISCOVERING THAT BUYING IN BULK IS A WAY OF SAVING MONEY. IN MOST INSTANCES THIS WILL REQUIRE A SEPARATE ROOM, OR PART OF A UTILITY OR LAUNDRY ROOM.

ABOVE **A simple rack in a room adjoining the kitchen can help organize food storage.**

OPPOSITE **Food, such as canned and boxed goods, is often stored in the kitchen, but a separate pantry provides more storage, especially for bulk items.**

or homeowners. The space above kitchen cabinets is often wasted, but can be used for storage of lightweight bulk items such as paper goods. Other normally wasted spaces, for instance under a stair case, or in an odd corner, can be utilized as a pantry storage area. Pantry storage can be created between the wall studs on interior walls, and provide enough depth

for the storage of canned goods. If designing a new home or remodeling an old one, consider having the builder or cabinetmaker add in these customized pantry storage areas.

The ideal situation is a separate pantry room, or walk-in pantry. Many families are discovering

ABOVE LEFT **Cleaning supplies can be stored in cloth-style units that can be carried to the work area or that keep supplies within reach.**

ABOVE RIGHT **Add-on pullout shelves make use of the unused space under the shelves in cabinets.**

OPPOSITE **Simple cloth door hanger holds mops, scrubbers, paper towels and other cleaning supplies. Many door storage units are available to turn the back of a door into anything from pantry storage to the cleaning closet shown here.**

buying in bulk is a way of saving money. In most instances this will require a separate room, or part of a utility or laundry room. A bulk storage system can also be set up in a corner of the garage or in a basement. This requires only a simple storage rack which can range from strictly utilitarian to more elaborate systems.

Regardless of where or how the pantry is located, organization is important, with the pantry system suited to your lifestyle. Divide the storage into specific areas for paper products, canned goods, boxed goods, soft bag goods, as well as storage of small appliances or pots and pans — those items you use occasionally, but don't have the space for in your kitchen cabinets. The cabinets and shelving should match the specific areas. For instance, storage of bulk paper towels requires higher shelves than those for canned goods, and paper products can be stored in deeper shelves. Smaller items, however, will get lost in the back or on deep shelves. Adjustable shelving is a great helpmate in a pantry, enabling you to suit the shelving to your specific storage needs. Some vegetables and fruits, such as potatoes, onions, grapefruits and oranges, can be stored in a pantry if it is dry and cool. Store produce in open bins so air can circulate around the items. Check frequently and remove any molding or rotting foods. A sturdy table or countertop should be located in a pantry area to hold bags of purchased items as you bring them in for storage.

Pantry Storage Tips

Label any undated goods as to the date purchased and try to use within two years or by label date. Store new purchases to the back, always using the oldest first. Flour, corn meal and other grains and sugar must be stored in dry, clean containers with lids that will fasten tightly. Consider sealing around the lid and container with masking tape for a long-term, bug-proof seal. Store dry cereal in tightly sealed containers. Pasta can also be stored in tightly sealed containers and even used as kitchen décor. Consider a vacuum packing machine. Storage times on many packaged foods can be increased if vacuum packed.

OPPOSITE **A well-organized pantry with plenty of shelving.**

RIGHT **Racks mounted to the inside of a closet door and inside the closet turn it into a pantry.**

LEFT Limited wall space can still be used to store things at arm's reach.

BELOW LEFT Even simple plastic basket slide-outs can help organize supplies.

BELOW RIGHT A clever pullout spice shelf.

OPPOSITE Rev-A-Shelf Pull-out pantry can be a part of the kitchen design, or in a separate room.

LABEL ANY UNDATED GOODS AS TO THE DATE PURCHASED AND TRY TO USE WITHIN TWO YEARS OR BY LABEL DATE. STORE NEW PURCHASES TO THE BACK, ALWAYS USING THE OLDEST FIRST.

Bathroom

Bathroom designs run from the utilitarian to "glam." Regardless of the appearance, the storage your bathroom offers makes the real difference. Bath and body supplies, towels, medicinal and first-aid supplies, along with cleaning products, often create an unorganized and cluttered storage problem and a bath that is impossible to keep neat and clean. Replace your old cabinet-style vanity with a modern pedestal lavatory and storage becomes even more of a problem. Fortunately, a wide range of bath organizing products is available. Bath solutions range from simple towel bars and hanging pegs to decorative and utilitarian shelves and a number of over-the-toilet storage products. There is also a variety of shower caddies available that can remove a lot of vanity-top clutter.

Bathroom Storage

The first step in organizing your bath is to examine it carefully for any unused space that can be turned into storage, including hallways. Adding cabinets is the first step. These can be medicine cabinets or kitchen-style wall cabinets. Many medicine cabinets are in-wall, fitted between the studs. A new, larger, surface-mounted cabinet can provide more space, and replacing the old with new is fairly simple. In-wall cabinets are held in place with screws through their sides into the wall studs. Remove these screws and pull out the old cabinet. A larger cabinet, however, can be quite a bit heavier. Have someone hold the cabinet in place, placing it at a height that best suits your family's needs. Use a level to assure the cabinet is level, and then anchor the cabinet in place with screws through the cabinet back and into the wall studs.

LEFT **The addition of a simple rack on the wall is an inexpensive way to add bathroom storage space.**

ABOVE RIGHT **A wire shelf can hold a necessary bathroom items and provide space for using clothes hangers.**

RIGHT **The Vanity Grooming Pull-Out from Rev-A-Shelf is designed for vanity base cabinets and comes complete with adjustable shelves and two stainless steel bins for storing curling irons and hair dryers.**

In many instances the vanity may have only a single drawer or a partial cabinet. A full vanity, with lots of drawers provides a great deal more storage. You may even wish to replace a pedestal-style lavatory if you need more space. Vanities are also constructed with pull-outs, similar to kitchen base cabinets. Rev-A-Shelf has created a cabinet that transforms decorative fillers into storage pull-outs. This allows you to utilize the space behind decorative fillers. The adjustable shelves feature clear polycarbonate rails and non-skid vinyl shelf liners. Clear acrylic storage trays are also included to keep smaller items organized. The 26-inch version for vanity height applications and a 30-inch base height version are available in three- and 6-inch widths. All are 19-inches in depth and have full-extension ball-bearing slides. Rev-A-Shelf Vanity Grooming Pull-Outs are designed to replace a full-height vanity door cabinet with easily accessible pull-out.

Beneath the vanity is often a cluttered and sometimes dangerous storage situation. Cleaning products should not be kept beneath the vanity if children are in the house. One way of adding more storage space is to utilize the space between the studs in the walls for cabinets. A floor to ceiling, between-the-studs cabinet can provide a lot of space. This should, of course only be on interior walls. Exterior walls hold insulation. It's also important to make sure no electrical wires run in the spaces desired for cabinets. Although this space is typically only 3½-inches deep, it can still hold such things as toilet paper, cleaning, and bath and beauty supplies.

Another method of organizing storage, if you have the space, is to place a free-standing cabinet, or armoire in the bathroom, or in a hallway next to the bathroom. These can not only provide lots of storage space but add to the décor as well. The size allows for storing extra towels and other bulky items.

Open shelving can also add storage space to bathroom walls. Free-floating or shelf-standard shelves are available in a wide range of types, styles and sizes. They are fairly easy to install, following manufacturers instructions. A number of decorative shelf systems are available, or you may wish to have a shelf custom made to fit a particular area.

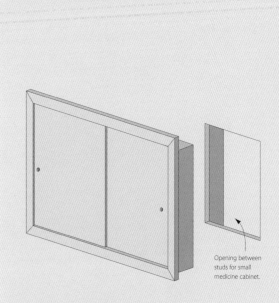

Opening between studs for small medicine cabinet.

ABOVE **Medicine-type in-wall bathroom cabinets that fit between the studs can be replaced with larger cabinets placed over the wall covering and anchored to the studs. Replacing these cabinets can provide a great deal more storage for medicines and first-aid supplies.**

LEFT **Small decorative shelf can hold a number of necessary bathroom items and add to the bathroom décor as well.**

OPPOSITE **After-market wire "drawers" make unused storage space easily accessible.**

ABOVE **Not all storage is enclosed. Place items in wire shelves for easy access.**

RIGHT **Free-standing cabinet in a near-by hall could be your answer for needed bathroom storage. A cabinet with both open shelves and drawers will hold decorative and functional items.**

LEFT A hallway linen closet can be used to store many of the items usually stored in the bathroom.

BELOW This small rolling rack can provide needed bathroom storage in even the smallest hall.

ONE WAY OF ADDING MORE STORAGE SPACE IS TO UTILIZE THE SPACE BETWEEN THE STUDS IN THE WALLS FOR CABINETS. A FLOOR TO CEILING, BETWEEN-THE-STUDS CABINET CAN PROVIDE A LOT OF SPACE.

Bedrooms

Most of us spend almost half our lives in our bedrooms. A bedroom can be a place for many things in addition to resting and sleeping. Bedrooms often serve as dressing rooms, home offices, even entertainment rooms with exercise equipment, books, music, internet access and television. Like most other rooms, organization can make a great deal of difference in how we enjoy our bedrooms, and how peaceful our place of refuge can and should be. Bedroom organization can take many different approaches. In addition to the bedroom, the closets adjoining the bedroom are also important, and are covered in the closet chapter.

Bedrooms

In days past, storage of bedroom items was primarily in bedroom furniture, as closets were often small or non-existent. The first bedroom furniture pieces were simple chests and trunks. Well-designed bedroom furniture today can include a number of traditional pieces. Bedroom furniture, however, not only should be well designed to store specific items, but should also set the décor and mood of the room. Most commonly furniture pieces are purchased as a matched set, but mixing and matching can also provide an unusual eclectic bedroom style.

LEFT **Wire baskets and shelves are perfect for updating a bedroom closet.**

OPPOSITE **Cubbyholes are great for separating items so they can be found quickly and easily.**

Dressers and chests, as well as dressing tables were and still are extremely important. A wide range of drawer accessories is available for organizing dresser drawers to hold a variety of items.

Nightstands with drawers or shelves can also add storage space, especially for small items. Blanket chests were an old-time item that can still provide great storage for bedding. In days past many chests were cedar-lined for protection from insects and other pests. Chests or even open furniture pieces with decorative baskets can be

LEFT **Out-of-sight storage made easily accessible with clear totes designed specifically to fit under the bed.**

ABOVE **Storage totes come in a variety of sizes and colors to organize and store almost anything. Totes are especially handy in the bedroom to store out-of-season clothing and bedding. Choose a size and color to suit your needs.**

RIGHT **Free-standing modular closet and dresser combination units are the perfect solution for bedrooms with no closet, i.e., this converted loft room.**

IN ADDITION TO FREESTANDING BEDROOM FURNITURE PIECES, A NUMBER
OF OTHER DESIGNS CAN BE USED. ONE OPTION, IF REMODELING OR BUILDING
A NEW HOME, IS TO ADD CABINETRY TO THE BEDROOM.

placed at the foot of the bed for even more storage.

The old-fashioned armoire or wardrobe took up a lot of space, but many were also well organized to hold a variety of items. They often included hanging bars or hooks for clothing, drawers for accessories and shelves and other organizational means. In the days of high (or at least 9-foot) ceilings, many of these old furniture pieces were at least 8-feet high and were very large, heavy pieces of furniture. Television and sound system equipment can be placed on the shelves, but they must be sturdy enough to hold the

OPPOSITE **The ultimate in bedroom storage, these multi-sections include everything from hanging rods to shoes to cupboards and drawers. Everything is neatly organized, yet readily accessible.**

ABOVE **This easy add-on takes up almost no space yet will organize over a dozen ties or scarves and pulls out to easily make your daily choice.**

RIGHT **An insert divider turns a drawer into a convient jewelry box.**

equipment. A better choice is an open or enclosed entertainment center built specifically to hold these items.

In addition to freestanding bedroom furniture pieces, a number of other designs can be used. One option, if remodeling or building a new home, is to add cabinetry to the bedroom. This has become increasingly popular, with upscale cabinetry again adding to the bedroom décor. You can design these built-ins to suit your bedroom lifestyle, including bookcases for those serious night readers. Modular storage walls, either open or closed designed, have also become increasingly popular. Many of these are available from manufacturers, often in kit-form, or in modular pieces that can be added together to create your own custom storage wall. Most are fairly easy to assemble, even for the inexperienced, and require little in the way of tools.

BELOW LEFT **This ultra-shallow drawer holds one layer of jewelry. Dividers include a ring storage section.**

BELOW RIGHT **Another convenient way to organize jewelry, especially longer necklaces and chains, is with the pullout hooks shown. Also, it will store a number of accessories including belts or scarves.**

OPPOSITE **This bedroom contains everything you need to organize your clothing and accessories including a convenient seat to aid in dressing.**

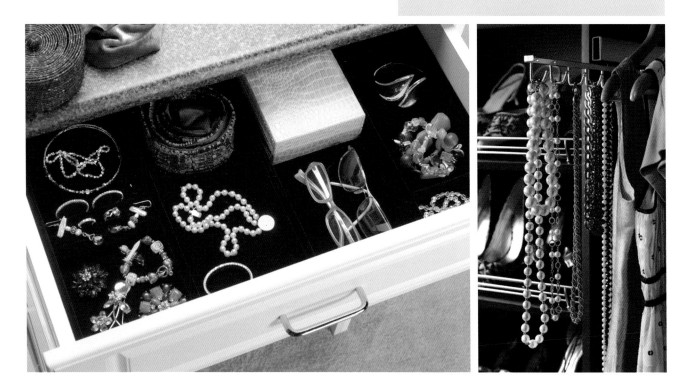

In addition to the traditional furniture pieces, and newer storage walls, there are other ways of finding and organizing storage in a bedroom. The first is the most obvious — under the bed. Any number of items can be stored under the bed, and a number of storage containers are designed specifically for sliding under beds. These can be used to store off-season bedding, even long rolls of seasonal wrapping paper. Some of the larger, heavier models are available with wheels for easier access. Make sure the lids fit tightly on these units.

Organizing and containing dirty laundry, or simply keeping clothes off the floor, is one common bedroom problem; but a very necessary one. Clothes strewn about the floor "breeds" even more mess. Decorative hampers are one choice; recycled chests and other furniture pieces can also be turned into laundry

OPPOSITE **Convenient wall system from ClosetMaid includes wall-mounted brackets and easily attached accessories. Shown is a pull-out clothes hamper with a shelf top.**

ABOVE **Drawer modular units are great additions to any bedroom. They add convenient storage for sweaters, lingerie and other more easily folded items.**

RIGHT **Long shelves attached to wall-mounted brackets make organization easy. See-through totes keep shoes clean and accessible.**

containers. In any case, you will need lightweight laundry baskets for transporting laundry to the laundry room and back to the bedroom. The old-fashioned coat or hat rack can be used to hang dressing gowns and robes when you're not wearing them, and it provides easy access. A common storage method in the past was a Shaker hanging rack with pegs to hold clothing and other items.

RIGHT **Open shelves hold totes, shoes and neatly folded T-shirts. Divided hanging units hold pants, skirts and blouses while a taller hanging area is provided for dresses.**

OPPOSITE **For the man who has everything, this combination of storage units will hold it all, from shoes to hats to laundry-folded shirts.**

ANY NUMBER OF ITEMS CAN BE STORED UNDER THE BED, AND A NUMBER OF STORAGE CONTAINERS ARE DESIGNED SPECIFICALLY FOR SLIDING UNDER BEDS.

Children's Bedrooms

Children's bedrooms and playrooms are where you can really have fun organizing. Kid's rooms are often a do-it-all situation. In addition to sleeping space, well-organized kid's rooms often have play areas, learning areas, exercise areas and lots of toy storage. A wide variety of items can be used to store toys, and this is where you can be creative. For instance, a pair of two-drawer file cabinets, a plywood piece for the top, paint and decals makes an economical and very effective desk. The main key, however, is making it extremely easy to store stuff. Even with a place for everything, children's rooms probably won't be the neatest rooms in your home. Having a place for everything, however, can help teach youngsters to put things up neatly.

Keeping It All Together

Organized closets are the first step. Colorful canvas boxes stacked on racks hold lots of toys, books and other items. Low shelves, in bookcase form, hold a lot of toys and they're easily accessible. Plastic crates can be stacked to create a modular storage wall. Mesh bags can be suspended from hooks to hold stuffed toys and bulky items such as volley or basketballs. Bunk beds can be used for two family members or as a guest bed. Kid's beds, with pull-out drawers, create storage in limited space. Loft beds also create more floor space for playtime. Some of these units come with built-in desks, book and toy storage areas as well.

LEFT **A wide range of organizational shelves, boxes, baskets and accessories is available. They can be used in a children's bed or play room.**

ABOVE **Storing items under the bed in plastic tubs, boxes or even pull-out drawers saves floor space for playtime.**

OPPOSITE **Good organization in a kid's room begins with an organized closet. In this instance the closet does not have doors, creating better accessibility and hopefully prompting neatness.**

Family Entertainment

The old-fashioned "rec" room, or den, now more commonly called the "family" room, is often the focal room of a home. This room is a place to relax, play games, or enjoy television or music. This room is also often "party central" or a place to entertain. As with any room, organization is important.

This room is probably, next to the kitchen, the most-used room in your home. More than likely, your family and friends, your children's friends, PTA members, the soccer or softball team and who knows who else will gather in your family room. They will have meetings and eat food or they might throw down some sleeping bags and have an overnighter. So, if everything has its place, it makes clean up much easier and you can be ready for the next big "event".

Getting Started

It's a good idea to list your recreation needs and design organization for the items you commonly use. Often the television and sound system or home theater is the focal point of the room. It's important to locate the system properly for easy viewing and listening as well as accessibility. Today's flat-screen TVs, even the larger screen sizes, are much easier to locate than the older, bulkier models. For best viewing, the television screen should be at eye level when seated.

An entertainment center containing the TV and other electronics, as well as storage for CDs, videotapes and DVDs can not only organize all, but if it has doors can also

LEFT **Keeping items such as CDs and DVDs properly stored not only preserves them, but takes clutter out of the family room and allows you to easily find what you're looking for.**

OPPOSITE **Modular units can be mixed- and matched to store a wide variety of items. Cabinets with doors store and conceal some items while open shelves display your favorite collections.**

be used to conceal the clutter when you're entertaining. These centers may be free-standing furniture pieces, or built-in cabinetry constructed specifically to hold electronics.

Modular cabinets can also be used to construct an entertainment "wall" to hold electronics, books, and also display your favorite collections. These units usually come unassembled, but are fairly easy to put together. They offer the advantage of versatility because you can mix and match shelving, drawers, cabinets with doors and other organizational units. You can also utilize furniture pieces, and an armoire is often the choice. Regardless of whether they're a furniture piece, shelves or modular cabinets, they should be of sturdy construction to hold the equipment.

If entertaining is your game you'll probably need storage for drinks and some food as well as serving ware. Wine racks can not

RIGHT **Party central storage, utilizing modular cabinets, can organize party supplies and make entertaining much more enjoyable.**

BELOW **Any number of specialized boxes and tubs can be used to contain and organize a variety of small items.**

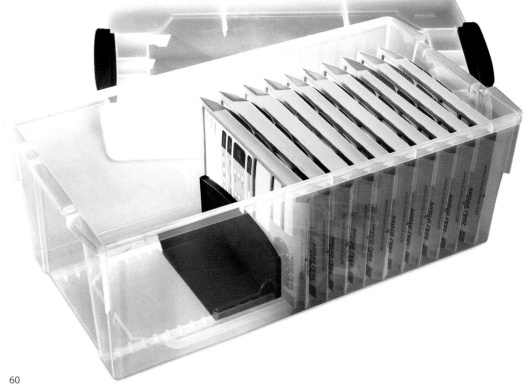

only serve as storage, but add to the décor of the room as well. A wet bar can definitely add to the convenience. Seating should be arranged comfortably, and one method of gaining more storage space is a hassock with a lift up lid. Tables with drawers can also add to the storage solution.

For some, curling up with a good book or magazine is a favorite pastime. Built-in or free-standing bookcases can be a major feature of the family room. If used to also display art or collections, they can in fact set the décor of the room. Display cases, both open and closed (with glass doors) can be a great addition to a family room and allow you to show off your favorite items and photographs. One popular design is a window seat with book, display shelves or cases built in on both sides of the window. If the seat has a lift-up lid or drawers, you can gain valuable storage for bulky items. A wide range of bookcases as well as "add-on" shelving is available. The latter can be easily attached to a wall. Regardless, it's

RIGHT **Pull out shelves and racks in cabinets make it easy to store and access party supplies.**

OPPOSITE **It's important to determine your favorite family-room use and design your room around the use. A pool table sets the mood of the room shown. Modular cabinets provide an entertainment center as well as a bar and storage for drinks and other entertaining supplies.**

important the cases or shelves be sturdily constructed, and, if free-standing, they should be securely fastened to the wall.

It's easy for growing families to accumulate a lot of games, and game storage is also important, not only to preserve the games, but to prevent clutter. Cabinets with deep drawers and closed doors are the best choice for storing board and other games.

With daily use, family rooms tend to be cluttered with books, magazines, newspapers, games and other items strewn about. But, if you organize your storage space to suit your favorite pastimes, you can cut the clutter and make your family room more enjoyable.

LEFT **In some instances a family room may also serve as a home office. A simple table and modular cabinetry and shelving create a "mini" office and computer work center in one corner of the room.**

ABOVE **Cabinets with doors can be used to store and conceal foods and other entertaining needs in the family room.**

OPPOSITE **Book and/or display shelves or cases are often an important feature of many family rooms. They can be free-standing or built-in.**

MODULAR CABINETS CAN ALSO BE USED TO CONSTRUCT
AN ENTERTAINMENT "WALL" TO HOLD ELECTRONICS,
BOOKS, AND DISPLAY YOUR FAVORITE COLLECTIONS.

Home Office

Home offices have become increasingly popular, not only as a place to take care of normal day-to-day business, but in some cases, a place to work from home as well. The computer age, with internet access, has made home offices a common part of most homes. The office may be part of another room, such as a bedroom, or in a separate room, but regardless of location, a working office that requires concentration should have some privacy and be away from the everyday hustle and bustle. If, however, the office contains a computer utilized by the entire family, the area should be located so parents can monitor computer use.

Setting Up

If part of another room, the working home office should be set up separately. One solution is a closet. Even a reach-in closet can be made into a home-office with pull-out or fold-down hardware and shelving or cabinetry. Actually you can create a home office in a closet easily and economically by using two, 28-inch high filing cabinets and a piece of MDF or plywood for the top. The 29- to 30-inch high desk, however, is too high for most people to efficiently use a computer keyboard. The solution is to utilize a pull-out keyboard holder fastened to the underside of the plywood desk top. Add shelves above for holding books and other supplies and you're in business. Another alternative is to utilize a simple table as your desk. Then place roll-around cabinets under the table. You can pull them out and access files or materials as needed. You will probably wish to have doors to close off the office as needed, but in some instances, if your office is simple and the shelving has space for displaying favorite decorative

LEFT **If your home office is one desk, then keeping most of your excess stuff in handy totes allows you to clean and organize the area at the same time. Simply get out the tote you need and store it back away when finished.**

OPPOSITE **A home office in a reach-in closet can be organized with many of the same shelves, drawers and cubbies found in clothing closets. The use of decorative boxes and bins along with the addition of a modern table used as the desk makes this office an attractive addition to the room.**

ANOTHER ALTERNATIVE IS TO UTILIZE A SIMPLE TABLE AS YOUR
DESK. THEN PLACE ROLL-AROUND CABINETS UNDER THE TABLE. YOU
CAN PULL THEM OUT AND ACCESS FILES OR MATERIALS AS NEEDED.

LEFT **A small shelf will add to
the décor of any room, even
a home office.**

RIGHT **This attractive home
office would fit into the
end of almost any room. A
freestanding computer desk
with a hutch top holds the
home computer equipment
while the opposite desk has
plenty of room to spread out
all your work, including your
traveling laptop.**

items, you might consider removing the closet doors for easier access and more floor space in the room. You might want to include a small fire-proof safe for holding valuable papers in your home office.

If you have guests infrequently, a corner or the closet of a guest bedroom might be considered for a home office area. A large armoire placed in a dining room, or other room can also be used as a home office. You can simply shut the doors to close off your office when not in use.

If you work at home frequently, or all the time, you should consider setting up a dedicated home office in a room by itself. Not only can this help with business taxes, but it provides more privacy for working and larger storage areas for books, research materials and other office supplies.

The first step in setting up a home office these days is set up the computer station. Numerous computer desks or stations are available to hold a variety of equipment and do different jobs. Match the station to your needs. Good

lighting is important in a home office. The work station should be located where you not only have sufficient electrical power, but also to provide the type and amount of light needed. Add a comfortable chair of the correct height to match your work station.

Modular, unassembled units, consisting of shelving, cabinetry and other organizing items can be mixed and matched to create a home office to suit your needs. These units can be simple and utilitarian. However, a number of very elegant home-office furniture pieces and cabinetry are available. In either case, just the right desk to suit your décor and style is the first piece to choose for the office. Then build from the desk-design to complete your office decor.

LEFT **Modular, freestanding drawer/shelf units offer a great deal of storage space for the small office. Drawers keep all the little stuff organized while the shelves are made attractive by using colorful storage boxes.**

ABOVE **The addition of this shelf unit to a small den helps turn it into a guest bedroom when the sleeper soft is opened. The shelf contains everything necessary for guest comfort.**

OPPOSITE **A small office area can be nothing more than a shelf between existing cabinets. Desk shelf holds phone and laptop computer while upper shelf holds necessary items in attractive bins and boxes.**

THE FIRST STEP IN SETTING UP A HOME OFFICE THESE DAYS IS SET UP THE
COMPUTER STATION. NUMEROUS COMPUTER DESKS OR STATIONS ARE
AVAILABLE TO HOLD A VARIETY OF EQUIPMENT AND DO DIFFERENT JOBS.

⑦ Closets

A well-organized closet can make or break a bedroom. It's one of the most important design features of a bedroom. If you're planning a new house, or remodeling, one of the major steps you can take in bedroom organization is closet design and construction.

Also, you'll be less likely to overload or "stuff" an organized closet. Some of us will remember the classic Fibber Magee and Molly radio program, when Fibber would open his living room closet. The clanking and crashing of the contents of the closet spilling out would take twenty seconds of air time and the laughs would take another twenty seconds. Most of us can relate to this closet full of anything that needs to be out of sight.

Making Closets

Closets are constructed in one of two designs. They may be *reach-in* or *walk-in*. Reach-in closets are the most common, as they take up less space. Reach-in closets are normally from 24"- to 30"-deep. This allows for hanger room, yet clothing and other stored items are easily accessed. These types of closets are easy to construct and, when bedrooms are back-to-back, reach-in closets are commonly designed side-to-side; an economical and efficient use of space.

LEFT **These easily attached closet cubbies can hold shoes or folded clothing. They can also be attached to the wall brackets at any convenient level. Shown are cubbies below hanging rods, but they could also be attached over hanging rods for less accessible out-of-season storage.**

OPPOSITE **The closet arrangement shown includes a number of modular units including a small section of wall bracketed movable shelves, shoe cubbies, enclosed drawers and open and enclosed shelves.**

Reach-in closets may be small, with only one door, or larger with more than one door. One problem with some reach-in closets, especially the smaller-size, one-door closets of older homes, is the organizational design. Typically, they have a closet rod or two and a shelf over the top rod. Quite often one or both sides of the closet extend some distance past the door opening. This means reaching back into these areas past clothes and other stored items, making those areas not quite as accessible. One tactic is to store off-season items in these "blind-corners," or utilize them for organizing clothing by seasons. Another tactic is to move the clothes rods to the sides, with shelves over them. The back of the closet can then utilize shelves, drawers or other built-ins.

The type of doors utilized can also make a difference in ease of access to the closet. A standard swinging door takes up space from the bedroom, and is the least efficient. Pocket-doors slide back into the wall, providing easier access, but are more costly and harder to construct. Sliding or by-pass doors do not take up bedroom space, but allow access to only one half of the closet at

LEFT **Wall bracket attachments also include these drawers.**

ABOVE **This ultimate his-and-hers closet has room for everything. Any number of modular units can be put together to suit your needs and available space.**

WALK-IN CLOSETS OFFER MORE SPACE FOR STORAGE, AND THEY
CAN ALSO UTILIZE MORE ORGANIZATION PRODUCTS. WALK-IN
CLOSETS MAY BE SIMPLY LARGER ROOMS, OFTEN RUNNING THE
FULL LENGTH OF A BEDROOM.

a time. Bi-fold or folding doors, as well as accordion-style doors allow better access, and take up less bedroom floor space.

Walk-in closets, of course, offer more space for storage, and they can also utilize more organization products. Walk-in closets may be simply larger rooms, often running the full length of a bedroom, with storage on four sides. Other types of walk-in closets may be narrower, corridor style, with storage on both sides and the end. Quite often walk-in closets utilize built-ins. Basically you are unlimited in what you might build-in including open shelving, open cubbies, closed cabinets and drawers. The ultimate is cedar-lined walk-in closet. Not only does this provide lots of storage space, but the cedar acts as an insect repellent.

Organizational products really shine when it comes to closets. A wide range of products is available from simple metal racks

LEFT **These bracket-attached shelves are made even more useful with attractive baskets. Cloth lined baskets can be used to organize small, like items.**

ABOVE **Store small items in this plastic hanging container.**

OPPOSITE **This small closet features a center unit with cubbies and drawers and hanging rods on both sides. One side has a double rod for shirts, blouses, skirts or pants while the other side has one rod for dresses.**

RIGHT **These bracket-attached shoe cubbies hold a dozen pairs of shoes each while the top becomes an open shelf for other accessories.**

BELOW RIGHT **Bracket-attached open drawer slides out for easy access.**

OPPOSITE **These bracket-attached wire shelves have hanging rods and are arranged to hang short, medium and long items while the shelves provide storage for accessories.**

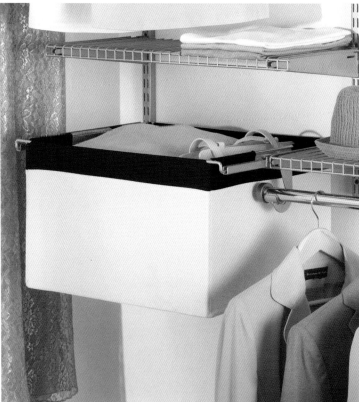

to complete built-in units. If you're planning a house, or remodeling, one of the major steps you can take in organization is closet design and construction. Regardless of whether you have or are constructing a reach-in or walk-in closet, it's important to organize your closets for maximum storage and easy access. Make a list of your items to be stored and then make up a sketch of how you would like to organize your closet. Figure at least three inches of closet rod space per clothing item, although most of us cram clothing much tighter. Closet rods should be spaced as either single or double. Top rods for double rod hanging, should be approximately 80 to 84 inches from the floor. Lower or bottom rods should be at 36 to 42 inches above the floor. Single rods for longer clothing should be from five to six feet above floor height. The

closet rod should be at least 12 inches from the back wall of the closet to allow for hanger space. If a shelf is to be added over the top rod, make sure it clears the rod by at least 6 inches.

One way of utilizing the top shelf space is to organize items in plastic tubs placed on the shelf. Another tactic for a top shelf, especially in a high-ceiling closet, is a pull-down closet rod, such as that from Rev-A-Shelf. Their new improved CPDR Series is available in three sizes to accommodate openings from 18 to 26, 26 to 35 and 35 to 48 inches. It feature a new and uniquely designed pivoting hub that allows the pull bar to be accessed from various angles, the innovative telescoping button locking pull-rod that allows you to adjust the length from 34 to 50 inches to accommodate use for universal design and handicap accessible applications.

Closet organizers range from simple shelf systems and various hanging racks to full kits. *A Visual Storage Planner* is a free-online

LEFT **The interior of this dressing room features a large, 8-drawer center chest complete with a seat.**

ABOVE **This free-standing cupboard can add a great deal of closet-type storage to your bedroom.**

OPPOSITE **An easy way to add seats for dressing to a smaller closet area is with hassocks as shown here. Hassocks that also offer storage would be best.**

tool from Closet Maid at www.ClosetMaid.com. It helps you design your space. After a quick download, you click to add components and when you're done, you have a design and parts list ready to print. ClosetMaid also offers a quick and easy affordable online design option. Complete a few questions regarding your storage area and needs, then ClosetMaid's team of design specialists will process your request. For a small fee, you receive two designs for a single storage space that includes line art drawings, color renderings, parts list and a where-to-buy option.

Most closet organizational products are easily installed, but a large closet will probably take a full weekend. Before you head to the home center, measure your closet and/or utilize the online storage planner. Following are the suggestions for a ClosetMaid system. The required installation tools include: Measuring tape, level, cordless drill, Phillips screwdriver and rubber hammer. You will want to have a few small dishes to keep tiny parts handy and organized. Choose an organizer kit with everything you need in one box, or create a custom design from open stock at the home center. Don't forget hanging tracks, standards and brackets needed. For the ClosetMaid ShelfTrack kits, start by installing the horizontal hang track to the wall. Then snap in the vertical standards at whatever width needed, but no more than 24 inches apart. (When you're finished, you can secure the standards to the wall.) Insert brackets into standards at desired heights and attach the shelving. If you want to change shelving heights, simply adjust the brackets and reattach the shelving.

OPPOSITE **These free-standing shelves can add storage in the form of an "open" or freestanding closet.**

ABOVE **Bracket-attached metal basket is also a slide out drawer. Arrange baskets on the wall bracket to suit your needs.**

RIGHT **This free-standing unit will work equally well in the closet or mudroom.**

ORGANIZATIONAL PRODUCTS REALLY SHINE WHEN IT COMES TO CLOSETS. A WIDE RANGE OF PRODUCTS IS AVAILABLE FROM SIMPLE METAL RACKS TO COMPLETE BUILT-IN UNITS.

If you're adding laminate components, like drawers and cubbies, assemble the accessories first. Then build the laminate tower units to hold the accessories and attach the drawer glides and door hinges. Finally, mount the towers on the ShelfTrack standards. Laminate pieces can also be mounted directly to the wall. Finally hang the closet rods to desired heights (usually 84 and 42 inches for double hanging, 70 inches for long hanging) and place the drawers and baskets.

RIGHT **This modular unit includes open shelves, shoe cubbies, drawers, a variety of hanging rods as well as a number of wire racks and baskets. Convenient bench completes the dressing area.**

BELOW **Another bracket-attached item, this shelf unit can be used to organize clothing or accessories.**

Garage/Shop

If your garage no longer has room for your car, you're not alone. Garages tend to collect a lot of stuff, some you need, some you probably don't. Organizing your garage may seem a daunting task, but sooner or later, you need to take back your car's space. This doesn't mean you can't store things in your garage, have a small shop or worktable.

Your garage can actually be a very versatile and highly functional part of your home. True, your automobiles use most of the space, but by simply moving your vehicles out of the garage, a large space immediately becomes available. This is where good planning and organizing will pay big dividends. Drop-down benches and tools on casters can instantly give you a working shop. Or, it can become a rehearsal studio for that up-and-coming garage band. Read on to see the possibilities.

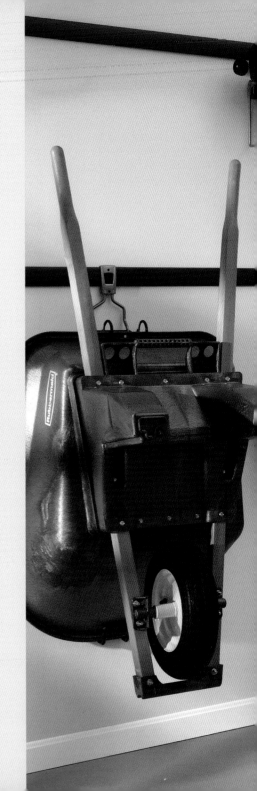

Cleaning Out and Organizing

Pick a warm, sunny weekend and have plenty of garbage bags, boxes, tubs and other ways of organizing gear. Sort the gear into piles of like items and then you can decide what to discard, recycle, donate or set aside for a garage sale. After you have decided what to keep, maintain the separate piles. For instance, you might have car care, home care, lawn and garden care and sports equipment piles. Store like items together for

OPPOSITE **These modular Craftsman units can be arranged to suit any work situation.**

RIGHT **The Rubbermaid FastTrack system also includes wall cupboards. The advantage is the cupboard is up off the floor, making cleaning easy.**

BELOW **A garage combined with a shop doesn't have to be a disaster. With plenty of organized storage a garage/shop can be both useful and organized.**

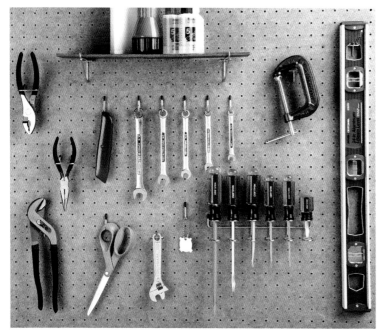

LEFT Pegboard was one of the first wall-hung organizers and can still be used to hang lots of tools.

BELOW An organizing wall system lets you hang any number of tools and equipment anywhere on the wall.

RIGHT A garage can incorporate kitchen-style cabinets with bracket-attached wall shelves to not only organize your stuff, but provide a great work area as well.

quick and easy location and access. Some items should also be stored well out of reach of children and pets. This includes poisonous supplies such as fertilizer, insecticides, herbicides, paints, thinners, and caustic cleaners. These items should be stored in closed and possibly lockable cabinets, or on high shelves. Make sure all chemicals are labeled, and check yearly, discarding those that have con-tainer damage. These items should also not be stored near a furnace, hot water heater or other heat source.

Items such as gasoline, white gas, diesel and fertilizer should also not be stored near each other. Fertilizer must be stored in a sealed container. A recycled bucket with lid or tub with a good sealing lid should be used. Store unused portions of potting soil bags in a closed trash can.

LEFT AND BELOW **The Racor wall shelf provides a work surface when you need it, yet folds out of the way when not in use. A great help for small garages.**

OPPOSITE **The Rubbermaid FastTrack system also includes bottom cabinets that not only provide storage and a work surface, but are also up off the floor for easy cleaning.**

You should also know whether items in your garage will freeze or not. A free-standing garage without heat should not be used to store supplies in glass containers, or paints and other materials that may freeze.

Plastic tubs, labeled as to the items stored inside can help organize a lot of smaller items, such as paintbrushes and other painting tools, and household maintenance supplies and tools, including electrical and plumbing. Another tactic is to have separate toolboxes for plumbing, electrical and other household repairs and maintenance.

LEFT Rubbermaid FastTrack system also includes solid and wire shelves attached to brackets. These shelves will easily adjust to store almost anything. A wire shelf on the bottom is great for wet and muddy shoes and boots.

ABOVE Slotted wall system is an efficient way to keep tools organized and easy to access.

OPPOSITE A freestanding cupboard makes a great, easily cleaned garage storage.

Pegboard and slotted wall systems to hold pegboard hooks can organize a lot of material and tools as well. Pegboard is relatively inexpensive, and easy to use, but slotted systems are more secure. One method of keeping gear organized with these systems is to paint an outline of the tool on the pegboard. This helps put items back in place. A number of wall-hung track systems are available with specialized hangers, baskets, bins and so forth for a wide variety of specialized items.

Organizing your garage is actually quite easy with any number of specialized organization products available, as well as ordinary shelving, cabinets and different types of wall hanging systems. Shelving and cabinets can be built-in or freestanding. If free-standing, make sure the shelving is secured to the wall. Lots of both free-standing and wall hung plastic cabinets designed specifically for garage storage are available. Modular units can be mixed and matched to create your own customized storage space, without a lot of custom building or effort. Many of these units are unassembled, but assembly is easy with a screwdriver, a set of wrenches and a rubber hammer. It's important the wall-hung units be secured to the wall studs according to the manufacturer's instructions.

You may wish to consider hanging items from your garage ceiling if you have the height. Simple hanging shelves can be anchored in place to hold bulky but lightweight items.

In many instances a garage also serves as a workshop, whether for car care, woodworking, or

often for both, as well as home maintenance chores. Proper storage of tools, parts and supplies is also important for a shop. Craftsman, as well as other companies, has numerous combination storage/workbench units that can be utilized in your garage. These include units for mechanics tools, as well as for general shop use. Storage benches on wheels, with a workbench top, can be rolled back under other benches or against a wall, and then rolled out in the garage when needed for work. Small items, such as screws, nails, nuts and bolts can be stored in recycled clear glass, or plastic containers, such as

BELOW **A Racor wall shelf unit is a very compact garage organizer. The closed unit shows two shelves and handy paper towel holder. Open reveals a third shelf and a work area.**

OPPOSITE **The wall behind the work surface features a bracket-attached system allowing you to hang tools or small items in baskets anywhere on the wall.**

IN MANY INSTANCES A GARAGE ALSO SERVES AS A WORKSHOP,
WHETHER FOR CAR CARE, WOODWORKING, OR OFTEN FOR BOTH,
AS WELL AS HOME MAINTENANCE CHORES.

those used for peanut butter, mayonnaise, jel-
lies and baby foods. Plastic containers work best
because they won't break if accidentally dropped
on the garage floor. If your shop includes stationary
power tools, such as a saw or drill press, they can
also be positioned on roll-around, locking-wheel
bases. Roll them out when needed and back
against the wall when not needed.

If possible, the shop should be a separate or
designated part of the garage, for instance along

RIGHT **Modular garage
units can be arranged
to create an instant
work area.**

BELOW **Racor garage
organizers grouped
together include a
trash bag holder and a
special wall rack just for
spray cans.**

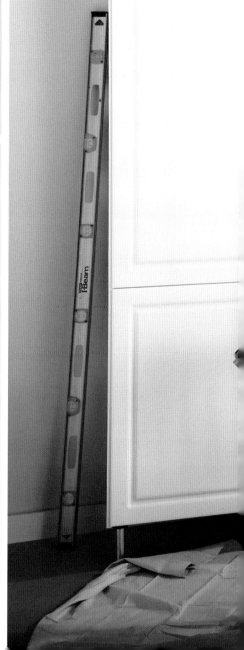

one wall or along the back if the garage is deep enough for both the automobile and shop storage and tools. One trick to make sure you don't drive too far into the garage and hit your shop is to suspend a tennis ball from the garage ceiling and just low enough to bump your automobile windshield when you pull in. If possible, the ball should be located so you have at least three feet between your car's front bumper and the shop area, in order to work at the shop with the car inside. Or you may simply have to leave the automobile outside when working in the shop area.

The garage is also a great place to set up a recycling center. A laundry basket makes a great place to collect old newspapers, magazines and other paper goods. Label three plastic garbage cans, with good fitting lids, for: Metal cans, glass and aluminum cans. Cut a hole in the top of the aluminum

BELOW **Recycling containers are conveniently located in this garage making recycling an easy, everyday job.**

OPPOSITE **Separate two-door cabinets to store all yard, garden and household chemicals is a great way to prevent accidents. Be sure to keep these items out of the reach of children. Locked is best.**

OPPOSITE BOTTOM **Close-up of the FastTrack hangers. Two hangers are used to hang a ladder.**

ORGANIZING YOUR GARAGE IS ACTUALLY QUITE EASY WITH
THE SPECIALIZED ORGANIZATION PRODUCTS AVAILABLE,
AS WELL AS ORDINARY SHELVING, CABINETS AND DIFFERENT
TYPES OF WALL HANGING SYSTEMS.

can holder big enough to drop the cans through, and position a can smasher just above for easy smashing and storage of aluminum cans. Rev-A-Shelf also has a great in-cabinet pullout to hold plastic waste cans and create a recycling center in a cabinet in the garage, kitchen or utility room.

Lawn and garden tools and supplies, as well as sports equipment is often stored in the garage, but it may also be stored in sheds and other buildings. The following chapter covers organizing and storing lawn and garden and sports equipment, both in the garage and in other buildings.

BELOW LEFT **Racor wall unit holds spray cans, but will also hold a readily-accessible flashlight.**

BELOW RIGHT **Separate two-door cabinet to store all yard, garden and household chemicals is a great way to prevent accidents. Be sure to keep these items out of the reach of children. Locked is best.**

ABOVE **Rubbermaid FastTrack hangers will hang almost anything up and out of the way.**

RIGHT **Rubbermaid FastTrack will hold any number of modular units including this free-hanging drawer unit.**

Garden and Yard, Sports

Garden and yard tools and materials can take up lots of space. The best way to store these items is in a separate building or shed. Lawn mowers, rakes, pots, potting soil, shovels, hoes, etc. can then be found easily if they are all in the same place. Looking for tools can be frustrating when you're ready to work. By the time you find what you've been looking for, you could be out of time and/or energy!

Sports equipment seems to multiply overnight. There's baseball gloves, bats, hats, shoes, uniforms, bicycles, helmets, gloves, first-aid kits and the list goes on.

All of this garden, yard and sports equipment gets dirty, which is another good reason to have a separate place to store it all.

Finding a Place for Everything

Lawn and garden as well as sports equipment is often stored in the garage, but sometimes these larger items are stored in a separate shed or building. These buildings may be permanent or portable. The former offers more storage space, the latter are not only more economical, but you can take them with you should you move.

Regardless of where the equipment is stored, a number of specialized racks, hangers and other organizational products are available. Or you can build simple shelves and

LEFT **This heavy-duty shelf unit not only holds a lot of weight, but also won't rust from water or chemicals. Four-shelf unit is easy to put together and holds a great deal of off-season yard necessities.**

OPPOSITE **Lawn, garden and sports equipment often takes a lot of space. A storage building or shed can be a great help.**

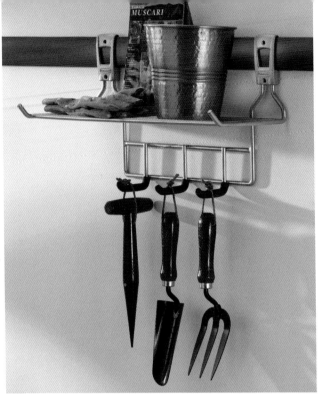

LEFT This small FastTrack attached shelf is specifically designed for flower garden tools and equipment.

BELOW Rubbermaid FastTrack Garage Organizing System makes organizing your garden and yard equipment quick and easy. After installing the track, attach a number of hangers, even shelves, to organize as needed.

RIGHT If gardening is your sport, work tables with rolling carts underneath, freestanding cabinet and Craftsman Versa Track sections on the wall will turn any wall into a garden center.

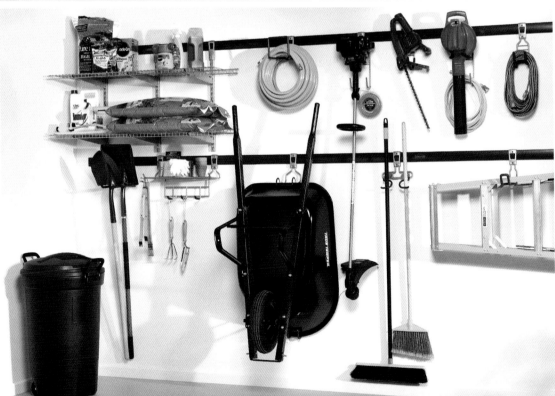

RACKS SHOULD BE USED TO HOLD LAWN AND GARDEN
EQUIPMENT, SUCH AS SHOVELS, RAKES, HOES AND OTHER
ITEMS TO KEEP THEM OFF THE FLOOR AND BEING A HAZARD.

place items on them, or in tubs or bins labeled as to the items contained.

We already discussed storing lawn and garden equipment in the garage, and the same organizing and storage tips and tactics can be used for storage in outside sheds. In areas subject to freezing, make sure you don't store liquids or other items that will freeze in these areas. Large plastic garbage cans are great for storing fertilizer, compost or potting soil. Racks should be used to hold lawn and garden equipment, such as shovels, rakes, hoes and others to keep them up off the floor and from being a hazard.

LEFT **Rubbermaid FastTrack can even be used to attach upper and lower storage cabinet units — with the bottom cabinet unit at a good working height.**

ABOVE **Outdoor storage container can be left on the patio to store many of your yard and garden needs right where you need them.**

OPPOSITE **Another method of organizing is with the tool tote shown. Soft-sided bags have been available for a variety of tools for some time and now are being designed specifically to tote around and store your flower garden tools.**

Sports

Sports equipment is often seasonal, bulky and hard to store. This includes ball equipment, water skis, snow skis, hockey gear, bicycles, canoes, golf clubs and camping gear. Bicycles and other items can be stored on hanging wall racks. Pool equipment, basketballs volleyballs, footballs and other items can be stored in a large mesh bag or even a recycled hammock hung in one corner of the garage. A wide range of cabinets and shelving is also available for holding these off-season items. If you have lots of small items such as fishing tackle, organize it in clear plastic storage boxes — labeled as to the contents. Guns and ammunition should be stored in a locked safe. It's a good idea to keep dehumidifying packets in with the guns.

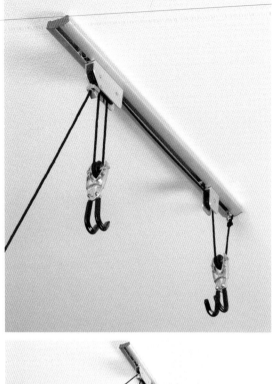

Skis, snowboards and other long, thin objects can be stored overhead in the garage or a shed on racks. Canoes, kayaks and small boats can be lifted up and stored overhead in a garage, if you have the ceiling clearance needed. A rope and pulley system on each end allows easy lifting. Small, lightweight boats and canoes can also be stored outside, turned upside down on sawhorses and covered with a plastic tarp. Larger boats take a great deal more care in storing for the winter season, especially if they are to be stored outside. Remove all electronics and move to a safe, dry storage area. Also remove any liquids, the fire extinguisher and all PFDs. The latter can be stored in cabinets or overhead in the garage. You may also wish to remove and store batteries inside. Do not store batteries on a concrete floor as it will zap the charge, and they should have a full charge before storing. If you don't remove the batteries, disconnect all electrical connections. Open all

OPPOSITE Ceiling-mounted rack allows you to pull a bicycle up to the garage ceiling for out-of-the-way storage.

ABOVE A wall can hold a lot of sports equipment that is then easily found when needed.

POOL EQUIPMENT, BASKETBALLS, VOLLEYBALLS, FOOTBALLS, ETC., CAN BE STORED IN A LARGE MESH BAG OR EVEN A RECYCLED HAMMOCK HUNG IN ONE CORNER OF THE GARAGE.

compartments and prop lids open to provide ventilation. Place a few mothballs in open containers around the boat to discourage mice, squirrels and other pests. Remove all tackle and rods. Unplug the trolling motor and coat the plug with anti-corrosion oil. Check the bilge and make sure all water is drained. Leave the drain plug out. Drain and check all livewells and cooler compartments. Wash and wax the boat and clean the upholstery. Remove portable fuel tanks, and treat fuel tanks with a fuel conditioner/stabilizer. Winterize your motor as per the engine manufacturer's instructions. Install a boat cover and make sure it is secured and taut.

Camping equipment requires a bit of maintenance and proper storage for the off season. Open and clean coolers, allow them to dry, then place baking soda inside to keep them smelling fresh.

Don't store a tent while damp or wet. Mildew will form, causing the material to rot or shorten the life of the tent. To kill the organisms, a mildewed tent should be left in the hot sun to dry. Keep tents stored in a rodent-free area.

Sleeping bags should be turned inside out, shook and then air-dried in the sun before storage. Again, do not store damp as they can mold and mildew. They should then be turned right side in, and stored in a warm, dry, rodent-free area. Sleeping bags store best hung over dowel rods in a closet or cabinet rather than rolled up. They'll stay dry and fresher for the coming season.

Thoroughly inspect all backpacks, remove dirt and debris from the pockets and inside the

ABOVE **Rubbermaid sports equipment rack will hold a lot of balls along with rackets and other sporting equipment.**

OPPOSITE **Several fishing rods and softball or baseball bats can be stored in a small space on the wall.**

bag. Make sure they contain no food material to attract mice and other pests. Store hung on a wall or in a large cabinet. Wash all camp kitchen utensils in a mild solution of bleach and water, dry thoroughly and store in a dry, secure place. Clean and check lanterns and stoves. Store kerosene stoves and lanterns, as well as fuel in an outside shed. Remove propane bottles from stoves and lanterns and store separately in a cool, dry place.

Campers require quite a bit of effort in proper off-season storage. The first step is to remove all food liquids. Drain the water tank, toilet and lines, and then use an RV winterizer to prevent freezing. Remove all foods, including canned goods. Foods can attract mice and mice can do a tremendous amount of damage over the winter. Make sure all openings are closed off. Placing containers of mothballs in the camper will discourage mice and pests. Remove or store steps and other easy access places to the camper. If the camper has a carbon-dioxide monitor, remove the battery or fuse. Make sure all windows and doors are properly shut.

Follow all manufacturer's instructions on storing ATVs, snowmobiles and jet skis.

⑩ Seasonal Storage

Storing off-season items is often the most challenging. This can include holiday decorations, off-season clothing, winter comforters and other bedding, luggage and travel items, food canning and freezing supplies, and sports equipment, including boats, snowmobiles, ATVs and campers. Each category offers specific challenges.

For example, Christmas decorations can include: A tree, tree stand, ornaments (usually several boxes), lights (for the tree and the house), decorations for the house, wrapping paper, ribbon, tape, etc. The problem is these come out once a year. Where do they go for the rest of the year? And, you want to be able to get to everything at the same time.

Let's take a look at some clever and efficient solutions.

Holiday Storage

Depending on the amount of decorating and your collection of holiday décor, storage can be a large problem. If you're a serious decorator for Christmas, Easter, Valentine's Day, Fourth-of-July, Fall, and Halloween, you'll have lots of items from small to very large and need lots of space. Serious decorators have an entire room for storage of these once-a-year items.

LEFT **Since your artificial Christmas tree spends most of the time in storage, it pays to store it right. Zippered bags are available to fit most trees. These bags will not only keep your tree parts together, but also keep it clean and protected for years.**

OPPOSITE **If you only keep a minimum of gift wrap and bags then these two containers are what you need. Tall container holds several rolls of gift wrap while the hanging tote holds a selection of gift bags.**

These off-season items can also be stored in closets, basements, overhead in garages or on garage racks. One factor to consider is as they are only used occasionally, it's best to utilize storage that's a bit harder to access. This often means high storage, on the top shelves of closets, attics and other such areas. Even the normally wasted space above kitchen wall cabinets, can be used for this type of storage. On the other hand, many of these items are fragile and need secure storage areas. Plastic tubs with snap-on lids are great for storing many of these items, with special tubs designed just for holding Christmas tree ornaments. Fragile items, such as statues, music boxes and dishes should be wrapped in foam before storage. If you have a number of tubs, organize each tub with specific items, such as wreaths, garland and so forth. A large plastic tub on wheels can also be used to store artificial Christmas or other holiday trees. Write the contents on the tubs with a felt-tip marking pen. Each year go through decorations and discard broken or non-working light strings and any other non-used items. Doing this each time the items are used and again before storing will greatly cut down on wasted space. Don't forget to make a list of the replacement items needed for the next season.

Wrapping paper and bows can be stored in flat, long plastic boxes that slide under a bed. You may wish to create a special wrapping area to hold paper, bows, tape, scissors, pens, cards and other necessary items. An old desk can be recycled into a wrapping center. Or utilize a custom-built cabinet with a large top for wrapping gifts.

BELOW **This specially made ornament box with straight sides comes complete with a front handle and label holder. A number of these boxes would fit on a shelf, yet be easy to find and grab the right box.**

OPPOSITE TOP **Totable carriers with labels can be stored almost anywhere.**

OPPOSITE BOTTOM **Stackable, clear plastic containers are ideal for holiday decorations.**

Holiday
Ornaments

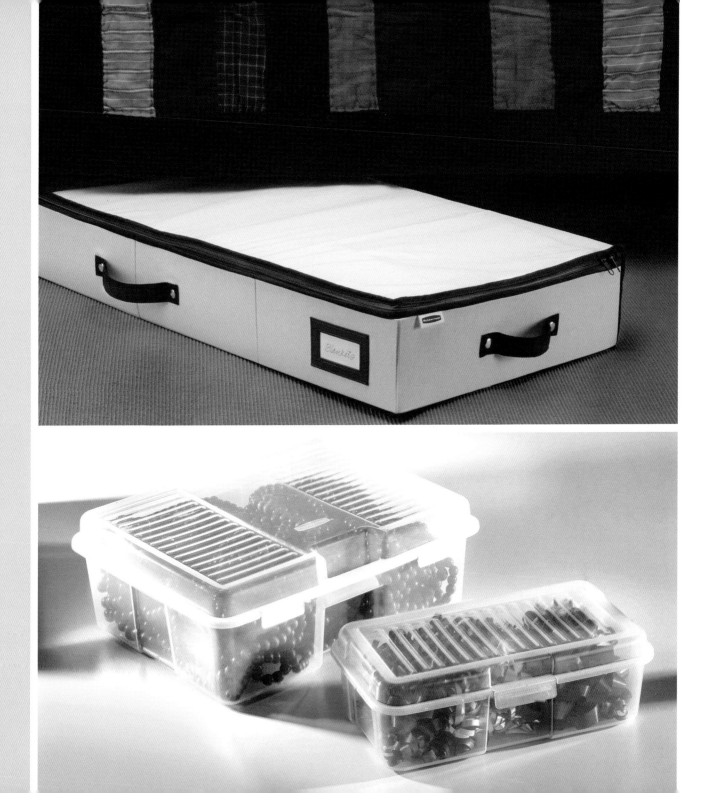

Laundry

A mud and/or utility room not only can be used for organizing shoes, coats, caps and other gear, but can help keep the rest of the house clean. Wet, muddy boots and clothing can be stored and hung to dry. A mud/utility room can also serve as a laundry and a small butler's pantry with a little organization. Using any extra shelves in your utility area for storing over-size and/or seldom used cooking pots, dishware and silverware can help cut down on kitchen clutter. The mud room, utility room, laundry room and back porch often utilize the same area. If so, creative organization is a must and you may wish to consult an interior designer or remodeler.

Multi-Use Room

Perry Szpek, a design sales consultant for JDJ Builders in Milwaukee, WI recently created more storage for a family of six by reconfiguring two existing rooms and adding some square footage. The family's mudroom was once a cramped hallway that led from the house to the garage. "Not having a place to put on and take off their shoes was their biggest pet peeve," Szpek said. As a solution, he designed two furniture-style storage units that provide both seating and a place to store outdoor gear. On one side of the room, a large boot-bench and locker cabinet gives the kids a place to sit down or hang up coats. The bench features storage beneath the seat and wicker baskets on a shelf above the hanging area. Drawer cabinets also flank each side of the bench, creating a personal spot for each child to stash hats, gloves and mittens.

Across the room Szpek planned a shorter boot bench for mom and dad that offered flip-top storage under the seat and hooks to hang coats behind them. Both storage pieces were accented with traditional beadboard backing, crown moulding and a medium-brown, distressed birch finish.

In the family's 120-square-foot laundry room, Szpek created a beautiful and storage-smart workspace. Upper and lower cabinets provide plenty of storage for detergents, brushes and sponges, and a long countertop gives mom ample space to fold clean laundry. Under one area of the counter, Szpek designed cubbies that accommodate six laundry baskets — one for each member of the family. When mom's done folding clothes, she can separate the loads into a separate bin for each member. The abundance of storage space worked great for this family of six.

OPPOSITE TOP **A laundry room can be an entire room or these simple adjustable shelves that will hold everything needed and use the wasted space over the washer.**

OPPOSITE BOTOM **A simple shelf can be a great addition to your ironing area. Not only will it hold your iron and supplies, but also has a place to hang your freshly-ironed clothing.**

RIGHT **A built-in laundry features a pull-out hamper with plenty of ventilation for even wet towels. Note the clean towel storage above.**

Often the laundry room gets little attention, but organizing storage can go a long way towards creating a more pleasant atmosphere for a job that is rarely enjoyed. Adequate cabinets are the first step. If your laundry room is drab and unexciting, consider revamping with brighter paint and a bit of décor. Cabinets and/or open shelves should be located so laundry necessities are ready at hand. A table or large countertop for folding and sorting clothes is also an appreciated feature. You may wish to incorporate a built-in ironing board, storage for a folding ironing board or a small sewing area for repairing clothing, sewing on buttons and other necessary chores.

Finding Additional Storage Space

Does it seem like you have too much to store in too little space? If you're like many homeowners, finding enough storage space can be a challenge. Remodeling professionals can help you create new ways to tuck away your family's treasures in a resourceful and sophisticated way, according to the National Association of the Remodeling Industry (NARI).

Finding storage solutions doesn't always mean undertaking a major remodel. Sometimes it's about using the square footage you already have. Remodelers can help plan and reallocate storage to accommodate your family's changing lifestyle. Getting creative with storage can improve daily living and boost the resale value of your home.

LOOK IN UNUSUAL SPACES

Veteran remodeler Don Van Cura, owner of Chicago-based Don Van Cura Construction, recently won a regional CotY Award for a clever storage solution he designed for stashing canned goods under a kitchen staircase. "I'm a space freak and I don't believe any part of the house should be wasted," he explained. "Almost every section of a home has a void in it that can be made into storage — and the older the house, the more nooks and crannies you can find."

For his stair solution, Van Cura created storage bins under the wooden treads of a staircase. He did this by attaching each tread of the staircase to the frame using hidden piano hinges, which allow each tread to open like a storage chest. The

ABOVE **This remodeler-created mudroom is the ultimate in organization and convenience for a family with busy children.**

OPPOSITE TOP **These steps created a wasted space in this small kitchen.**

OPPOSITE BOTTOM **Veteran home remodeler Don Van Cura turned the steps into clever storage for dry and canned goods.**

homeowner could then use the space under the tread to tuck away dry goods and cans. This storage strategy can be used in many areas of a home. In the foyer, for example, the hidden cubbies under the stairs could hold shoes and outdoor gear. In the basement they can store cleaning supplies or seasonal accessories. For a short run of stairs, remodelers can also install a set of custom drawers underneath the stairwell with access from either the side or the back, another great use of space.

Any good stair installer or skilled remodeler should be able to do this project, but it demands a structurally sound staircase, fine cabinetry skills and careful preparation. "It's easiest if you're planning a new set of stairs, but it can also be done as a retrofit to existing stairs," Van Cura notes.

Attic & Basement

Two traditional and common storage areas include the attic and basement. Both can have problems. An attic can be extremely hot or cold and basements can be damp, causing mold problems. Both, however, can be used for off-season storage with proper planning. It's important to make sure the ceiling joists in the attic will support the extra weight. The attic can have planks installed over the open ceiling joists to walk and store items on, but it's important not to cover electrical wiring or boxes. One easy way of covering is to use 2x4 tongue and groove panels, available at your local building center. Do not store flammable items in an attic, near a chimney or flue. Anything that can be damaged by heat or cold should not be stored in the attic. This includes water-based paints, photographs, slides, CDs, video or audio tapes, canned or bottled foods or any liquids that may freeze. To protect from pests place items in plastic tubs with tightly locking lids.

Basements usually have problems with moisture. Make sure the basement is well sealed with a waterproofing compound and the gutters and downspouts of the house are working properly. Even at that, high humidity may create problems and you may need to run a dehumidifier. Certain items should not be stored in these areas including paper goods, magazines, books, photographs and records. Clothing, shoes, and other cloth or leather items may also mold and mildew. Make sure all items are stored in sealed plastic tubs or bags and are off the floor.

ABOVE LEFT **Fold-away staircases are the best choice for accessing the attic crawl space over your home or above your garage.**

ABOVE RIGHT **Sometimes attic space can be remodeled to create a living space that is perfect for hobbies, gift wrapping and playing games.**

While some homeowners may think a bigger home will solve their storage dilemma, this is not always the case. Often, having better storage is about making better layout choices and putting things within easy reach. Before talking to a remodeler, homeowners should take a thorough assessment of the square footage they have and how much stuff they need to store. In addition, it's important to think about day-to-day schedules. Some areas of the home, like foyers or mudrooms, could use additional cabinetry or places to drop cell phones, keys and wallets. Sometimes the project is more about reworking the traffic flow or designating specific spots for tasks like folding laundry, putting on outerwear and storing cleaning products.

NARI Certified Remodelers can help homeowners plan smart and attractive storage for any size home. Visit www.RemodelToday.com to find a remodeler in your area.

Even if you don't have a finished garage with a ceiling, you can still have plenty of "up" storage. This same tactic works with garden sheds and other buildings, with open framing or trusses, even without a finished ceiling. First, determine what you wish to store. For instance seasonal tools, such as snow shovels, tree pruners and other long-handled tools can be stored above the ceiling joists. This is also a good place for maintenance materials, such as extra pieces of guttering or a few replacement pieces of exterior trim or siding. Another tip for finding storage with an open-truss building is to screw 2x4s across the trusses. It's amazing what you can store in this manner, from water and/or snow skis to empty coolers.

Hobby Rooms

Indoor hobbies include quilting, scrapbooking, fly-tying, painting or art crafts, building models and more. If you can devote an entire room to your family's hobbies, great. However, most hobbies utilize an area or space of another room or corner of the bedroom or laundry room. Your hobby space must be organized and the less space the space, more organization is needed. If your family has several hobbies, an entire room should be devoted to the hobbies, with work stations for each hobby.

Most hobbies require storage for lots of items, often many small items. Materials and sewing notions can be stored on purchased racks. Small, clear-plastic boxes are great for holding small items, such as sewing thread and no-tions. They can be labeled and placed on shelves for easy access. Painting and art supplies, especially paints, should be stored in a cool/dry area, with small brushes stored upright in jars or similar containers. A closet can be converted into a storage area and a closet organizer can be used to great advantage. Drawing paper, pads and canvases should be stored flat on a surface.

A rolling cart with drawers or several shelves is handy for artwork. The top of the cart can hold brushes and water or brush-cleaning materials. Drawers can hold paints, supplies and the shelves for paper storage. Roll the cart to your easel or work table and roll it into a closet when finished. Small plastic bins can be used to hold other craft items, again labeling them and plac-ing them on shelves. A desk can be a work area at either sitting or standing height with a pegboard above the desk for tool storage. A folding table is perfect for cutting materials from a pattern.

The room or area should be comfortable, conducive to relaxing with your hobby. And, they should be well lite. Artists prefer a North window for that famous North light. Tedious hobbies, such as fly-tying require a good desk-type light source.

ABOVE **If quilting is your hobby, this easily put together open cabinet will organize your collection of materials.**

OPPOSITE **By turning your guest room closet into a sewing storage area, you can have your hobby and your guest room. Simply fold the sewing table into the closet and close the doors when company comes.**

IF YOUR FAMILY HAS SEVERAL HOBBIES, AN ENTIRE
ROOM SHOULD BE DEVOTED TO THE HOBBIES, WITH
WORK STATIONS FOR EACH HOBBY.

Prepared for Emergencies

Floods, hurricanes, tornadoes, ice and electrical storms can all create emergencies, not to mention the cuts, scrapes and other injuries that are an everyday part of life. Being prepared for emergencies, big or small, is essential for any family. Having a special area to hold emergency equipment and supplies not only helps organize, but makes it easier to find things needed in a hurry.

A cabinet or cabinets in a mudroom, porch, garage, basement or other area and used only for emergency supplies is a good idea. Regardless of the location, it should be readily accessible. Modular cabinets can be used to create the storage space you need. Then make up a list of emergency supplies and equipment needed. You should have bottled water, canned or non-perishable foods (along with a can opener), flashlights (with spare batteries), fire extinguishers, candles, matches and of course a well supplied first-aid kit. A weather radio that operates on a battery and is kept charged should also be included. Some radios can be powered with a hand crank that will also charge your phone. A propane stove and lantern can be a great help when the electricity is out, but only use these items in well-vented areas. Spare cooking pots, pans and plastic eating utensils will help. First-aid manuals are a good idea. Post emergency numbers on a chart taped inside a cabinet door. You may also wish to include boots and warm clothing for each member of the family along with sleeping bags.

Make a list of the supplies and equipment stored and check the supplies every six months. Write the purchase date on food items without a use-by date and use within a year. To keep from throwing away outdated items, rotate all food and batteries before expiration by using the older and replacing with new. Emergency supplies shouldn't get too hot in the summer or freeze in the winter. If you have a storm shelter or basement, keep your emergency supplies where you will most likely be in an emergency.

OPPOSITE **Modular or kitchen-style cabinets can be used to create an emergency center.**

Suppliers

CLOSETMAID
www.closetmaid.com
ClosetMaid's products are available at most home improvement retailers and from an extensive network of installing dealers in the home building industry.

BEST BUY
www.bestbuy.com
Organizational products for the home and home office

CANADIAN TIRE
www.canadiantire.com
Department store, organizational products for the home and home office

CRAFTSMAN
www.craftsman.com
The full line of Craftsman products is available at all Sears stores and a select assortment of Craftsman products is available at any Kmart store. To purchase Craftsman products, use our store locators to find a Sears or Kmart store near you.

CVS PHARMACY
www.cvs.com
Prescription drugs, home health care and organizational products for the home

THE HOME DEPOT
2455 Paces Ferry Rd. NW
Atlanta, GA 30339
800-430-3376 (U.S.)
800-628-0525 (Canada)
www.homedepot.com
Home improvement supplies and organizational storage products for the home

K-MART
www.kmart.com
A complete line of rganizational products for the home and home office

LOWE'S COMPANIES, INC.
P.O. Box 1111
North Wilkesboro, NC 28656
800-445-6937
www.lowes.com
Home improvement supplies and organizational storage products for the home

MENARDS
www.menards.com
Home improvement supplies and organizational storage products for the home

MEIJER
www.meijer.com
Has a complete line of organizational products for the home

OFFICE DEPOT
www.officedepot.com.com
Has a complete line of organizational products for the home and home office

OFFICE MAX
www.officemax.com
Organizational products for the home and home office

PAMIDA
www.pamida.com
Wide variety of merchandise, organizational products for the home

RACOR, INC.
955 National Parkway
Suite 95500
Schaumburg, IL 60173
800-783-7725 Toll-free
www.constantines.com
You can find our products at thousands of retail outlets all over the U.S., Canada, Europe and Australia along with hundreds of secure web stores.

REV-A-SHELF
www.revashelf.com
The product line currently consists of polymer, wire, wood and stainless steel components, manufactured and marketed globally to kitchen dealers and furniture manufacturers, cabinet industry distributors and retail home centers.

ROCKLER WOODWORKING AND HARDWARE
4365 Willow Dr.
Medina, MN 55340
800-279-4441
www.rockler.com
Woodworking tools, hardware and books

RUBBERMAID
www.rubbermaid.com
Rubbermaid products can be found almost everywhere including mass retail, hardware and home center stores, warehouse clubs, supermarkets, drug stores, department stores and specialty stores.

SAUDER
www.sauder.com
Complete line of RTA (ready to assemble) furniture. Use our dealer locator to find a store near you.

SEARS
www.sears.com
Craftsman products, a complete line of organizational products for the home

TARGET
www.target.com
Has a complete line of organizational products for the home

WALMART
www.walmart.com
Department store, carries a complete line of organizational products for the home

WOODCRAFT SUPPLY LLC
1177 Rosemar Rd.
P.O. Box 1686
Parkersburg, WV 26102
800-535-4482
www.woodcraft.com
Woodworking hardware

WOODWORKER'S SUPPLY
1108 N. Glenn Rd.
Casper, WY 82601
800-645-9292
http://woodworker.com
Woodworking tools and accessories, finishing supplies, books and plans

Photo Credits

title page, ClosetMaid (CM)

page 4

   upper, Rubbermaid (RM)

   lower, CM

page 4, CM

pages 4-5, CM

page 5,

   upper RM

   lower photos, Rev-A-Shelf (RAS)

page 7, CM

page 8,

   left, RM

   right, CM

page 8 & 9, CM

page 10, RM

page 12, RM

page 13, photos 1-4, RAS

page 14, all photos, RM

page 15,

   left upper & lower, RAS

   right upper & lower, RM

page 17, RM

page 22, RM

page 23, CM

pages 24-25, all photos, RM

page 26, CM

page 27, RM

page 28, all photos, RM

page 29, RAS

pages 30-31, CM

page 32, RM

page 33,

   upper, RM

   lower, RAS

page 34, RM

page 35, CM

pages 36-37, all photos, RM

pages 38-41, CM

page 42, both photos, RM

pages 43-44, RM

page 45, CM

   upper, RM

   lower, CM

pages 46-47, all photos, CM

page 48, CM

page 49,

   upper, CM

   lower, RM

pages 50-51, CM

page 53, CM

page 54,

   upper, RM

   lower, CM

page 55, CM

page 56, CM

pages 58-59, CM

page 60, RM

page 61, CM

pages 62-63, CM

page 64, CM

page 65, Sauder (S)

pages 66-67, CM

page 68, RM

page 69, CM

page 70, RM

page 71, S

page 72,

   upper, RM

   lower, CM

page 73, CM

page 74, RM

pages 76-77, all photos, RM

pages 78-79, RM

page 80, both photos, RM

page 81, CM

pages 82-83, all photos, RM

page 84,

   upper, RM

   lower, CM

page 85, RM

page 86-87, all photos, RM

page 88, RM

pages 88-89, CM

pages 90-91, RM

More great titles from Betterway Home and North Light books!

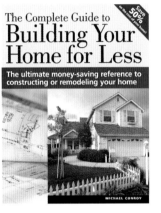

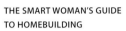
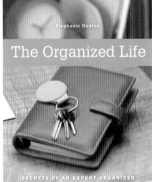